Morning Coffee with the Lord
By C.G. Harris

Morning Coffee With The Lord © 2011 CasSandra G. Harris
All rights reserved

ISBN 978-0-9852937-1-0

eISBN 978-0-9852937-0-3

Printed and bound in the United States of America. No part of this book may be reproduced or transmitted in any form or by any means, electronic or mechanical, including photocopying, recording or by an information storage and retrieval system, except by a reviewer who may quote brief passages in a review to be printed in a magazine, newspaper or on the Web, without permission in writing from the author. For information, please contact CasSandra Harris, 972-213-4033.

Although the author has made every effort to ensure the accuracy and completeness of information contained in this book, we assume no responsibility for errors, inaccuracies, omissions or any inconsistency herein. Any slights of people, places or organizations are unintentional.
First printing 2012

Library of Congress Control Number: **2012903982**

Library of congress Cataloging-in-Publication Data
Harris, CasSandra G.
  Morning Coffee With The Lord

Acknowledgements

There are a number of very special people that have inspired and contributed to my experience in writing this book.

My gratitude and love to my husband, Otis, who is my greatest encourager. Thank you for always believing in me. Your love and support is priceless.

To my children, Branden and Kristen, you are my greatest accomplishment and my secret Super Heroes. I will love you forever.

Thank you Bishop T.D. Jakes and Mrs. Serita Jakes. Your friendship and encouragement is monumental in my life. You both have helped me believe in achieving the impossible.

Thanks also to Rebecca Moore, Janice Robinson and Stephanie Freeman. You are each precious jewels. You are more than friends. You are my sisters. I will forever cherish your love and loyalty.

Dedication

In memory of my mother and my sister, Vivian Bryant and Toni Romelle Harris, who died before the completion of this book. Their confidence in me has been instrumental in my accomplishments. I will miss and love them forever.

Preface

Morning Coffee with the Lord will lead you on a journey of healing and restoration. Silence is broken. Hidden things are uncovered. You will be encouraged, inspired and motivated as you see snapshots of your life interwoven in each chapter of the book. You will gain an understanding of the purpose behind your life experiences and struggles. At last, you will find practical answers to help you navigate the challenges of everyday life.

Table of Contents

AUTHOR'S NOTE	9
I CAN'T QUITE PUT MY FINGER ON IT	11
JOY REALLY DOES COME IN THE MORNING	13
WHO ARE YOU GOING TO TRUST?	16
ITS JUST A SHADOW	19
IT'S NOT WHAT I THOUGHT IT WAS	24
HELP I'VE FALLEN AND I CAN'T GET UP	26
IDENTITY CRISIS	29
LORD I NEED A DO-OVER	31
JUST LIKE A HAMSTER ON A WHEEL	35
HOLIER THAN THOU	38
WHITE NOISE	40
STOP BACK SEAT DRIVING	42
FIVE MINUTES OF PRAISE	46
WHEN MY MIND IS FIXED ON JESUS	49

SEEKING HIM EARLY	53
PUT IT ON THE LINE	55
HOW DO YOU SEE HIM?	60
JUST DO IT	63
HAST THOU CONSIDERED MY SERVANT?	66
BECAUSE YOU FOUGHT	70
TIME IS RUNNING OUT	73
AFTER THE STORM	76
DON'T FORGET THE IMPORTANT STUFF	79
WHEN GOD IS SILENT, OR SO YOU THINK HE IS	82
LIFE IS LIKE A SEESAW	86
EYES WIDE OPEN	89
ARTIFICIAL GLORY	92
POSITIONING DOES NOT EQUAL SOVEREIGNTY	96
CALLED BY HIS NAME	103
THE LORD IS	109
NOTES	112

Author's Note

I do so enjoy having my morning coffee with the Lord. It is the time that I sit in the quiet of my living room talking with and listening to the Lord. During this time, it is the place where he reminds me of his love for me, breathes fresh ideas into me, reveals himself and gives me understanding and direction. It is a special time that is just for me.

Whether it is coffee, tea, juice or whatever your morning favorite might be, I encourage you to stop and enjoy it with the Lord. That brief time of sharing with the Lord will forever change your life. It was during these times that I obtained answers for my life. I gained an understanding of my purpose. I've always known what my purpose was, but I could never quite understand the how and why. That changed through morning coffee with the Lord. It was here that the Lord imparted wisdom, direction and gifts that are instrumental to my purpose. Books were birthed in my spirit as I sat quietly before Him. In fact, this book was given to me on the day I celebrated my birthday. The wonderful gift I received will continue to give to so many more.

As you read and reflect upon your personal experiences, I pray you will be both encouraged and inspired. Whether it's fifteen minutes or two hours, enjoy your morning coffee with the Lord. He is waiting to spend that very special time with you.

Chapter 1

I Can't Quite Put My Finger on It

Have you ever experienced one of those days where you were unsettled in your spirit and did not understand why? When you thought about it, you could not pin point anything in particular that was wrong. Everything was under control. Your loved ones were safe and sound. However, there was still an uneasy feeling in the pit of your stomach, a feeling of impending doom.

This is a perfect time to worship the Lord. Remember, he is the author and finisher of your faith. Know that the Lord will perfect everything that concerns you. Worship him in love. When you pray today, present him with all of your cares. Reflect back over the things the Lord has done in your life. You will be reminded of just how much the Lord cares about you. Remember to thank him for the angels that have been commanded to stand guard over you and your loved ones. Be at peace knowing that God has his hand upon your life and is watching over you.

The Lord shall preserve you from all evil: he shall preserve your soul. The Lord shall preserve your going out and coming in from this time forth and even forever more.
Psalm 121:7-8 NKV

Chapter 2

Joy Really Does Come in the Morning

Occasionally, life becomes overwhelming. There are times that you are so overloaded that you become exhausted mentally and physically. Nothing seems to be going smoothly and there is no immediate sign of hope or relief. You think about everything that is crowding your life, both past and present. You feel a cry in your spirit as you think to yourself that you have reached your tipping point. You know that you can't handle another thing without exploding. Secretly, you imagine what it would be like to stop the madness and just be with the Lord. Most of us will not admit that there have been times that we were just tired of the battles that come with life and there was no fight left in us. At some point, most of us have experienced this thought, even if it is a brief and fleeting moment.

Suddenly it happens; your morning comes. Unexplainably, you are refreshed and have a completely new perspective. Even though you still have the same challenges, you are filled with hope. Your challenges have now become new opportunities. Thinking about it, you realize that those issues that were plaguing you weren't as big as you had allowed them to become in your mind. What happened? You changed your perspective. When you are tired and over extended, a good night's sleep will give you a fresh outlook on challenges you must face in life. Yes, a good night's sleep. There are times that all you can do is tell the Lord your concerns and just go to sleep. More frequently than not, your problem is out of your immediate control anyway. If you could control it, it would not be a problem. After you have lost at the game of Tug-of-War, and you are at your wits end, the smart choice is to give it to the Lord and get some rest.

As you reflect over the low points of your life you will realize that a good night's rest always precedes your morning. It is okay to trust in the Lord and get some rest. Joy really does come in the morning.

It is a sign between me and the children of Israel forever, for in six days the Lord made heaven and earth, and on the seventh day he rested, and was refreshed.
Exodus 31:17 KJV

For I have satiated the weary soul, and I have replenished every sorrowful soul. After this I awoke and looked around, and my sleep was sweet to me.
Jeremiah 31:25-26 KJV

Chapter 3

Who Are You Going to Trust?

Can you remember the last time that you lost sleep worrying about a situation that was out of your control? We all have fretted over things that might or could happen. From time to time, we have all been in a situation that we simply did not have control over. For example, consider working for a corporation. Most companies downsize and layoff workers. At least this was true for the companies that I worked for. I survived all but one of the layoffs. I was fortunate enough to be notified in advance. Even though I knew it was coming, it was still a blow to my ego. After my position was eliminated, I went through all of the behaviors that one goes through when being told you have a terminal illness (Denial/Isolation, Anger, Bargaining, Depression and Acceptance – Elizabeth Kubler-Ross on Death and Dying 1969).

You may be in a position where your job is secure. Your career is on track and your world is great. With the stroke of a pen, you have been reassigned to report to a new manager.

In a very short period of time, you discover that you are working for someone who you are certain is Satan's first born. This manager is anointed to frustrate your life to levels you never knew existed. You are convinced that robbing you of your peace of mind and destroying your career is your manager's sole mission in life. Seemingly there is no way out. I can see you nod in agreement as you think about your own personal experiences.

I wish I could say that this has only happened once in my life. Unfortunately, that's not the case. However, I can triumphantly say that God delivered me each and every time. I have my share of battle scars and definitely endured frustrating situations for longer periods than I would have desired. The trials kept me grounded. I was forced to keep my eyes on the Lord, trusting him to intervene.

Don't you just hate it when you have to go the long way around the block to receive what the Lord is birthing in you? It is through these desperate situations that God refines our character and equips us for our destiny. If you are going to fulfill your purpose and do everything the Lord has called you to do, you will have to be trained through life's experiences to unconditionally trust in the Lord. As you look over the resume' of your life, you will find that the Lord has always been right there cheering and coaching you on to victory.

> *Some trust in chariots, and some in horses, but we will remember the name of the Lord our God.*
> *Psalm 20:7 KJV*

Chapter 4

It's Just a Shadow

I remember chasing my shadow as a child gazing in amazement at how tall my shadow appeared. To me, it was gigantic. I would chase it not realizing that it was I who was in control and not the shadow. My shadow was not something to be captured because the only power it had was the power I gave to it in my mind.

As adults, instead of chasing shadows we run from and fear them. The shadows of unfulfilled dreams and hurt in our lives lord over us. We allow the shadows of our past to infiltrate our minds with regrets and hopelessness. Focusing on the shadows distracts us from the very real present and promises for our future. Remember, it's just a shadow. It can't hurt or control you. The only power it has is the power you give to it when you meditate upon it.

Choose this day to flip on the light switch! Darkness has no place or power in the light. The light of the Son of God always overtakes the shadows that lord over our lives. Stop chasing the shadows and chase the Savior.

Yea, though I walk through the valley of the shadow of death, I will fear no evil: for thou art with me; thy rod and thy staff they comfort me.
Psalm 23:4 KJV

Chapter 5
Leftovers

I never really cared for leftovers. I prefer food that is served fresh and hot. It tastes best when it is freshly prepared. Warming food over or eating it over the next few days never tastes as good as when it was freshly cooked. The aroma of a freshly cooked dish can fill the house for hours on end. The aroma of a dish reheated pales in comparison to a freshly prepared dish. Freshly cooked food saturates the atmosphere.

There is something special about the first. Think about some of the firsts in your life, your first love, your first bike, your first car, first dance and so on. The first is always special. No matter how many years go by, those "first" moments create cherished memories in your life. You may get a new car or even a new love. It could be the car of your dreams and the love of your life, but it will never replace the fond memory of your first.

God feels the same way about the first. We often give him leftovers. Though it may be unintentional, we give God our left over time, money, prayers and worship. It doesn't feel good to admit it, but if we honestly reflect we will find that we have been guilty of presenting God our leftovers.

There are easy ways to recognize when you are presenting leftovers to God. Let's look at a few of them.

- Are you so busy that you don't make time to spend with the Lord? It gets easier to stay away longer and longer.
- Have you ever missed tithing? It gets easier to miss it again and again.
- When you give an offering, is it an act of worship and reverence of the Lord? Or, are you just giving because it was announced from the pulpit that it was time for the offering portion of the service?
- Do you read your bible out of obligation? Is it just another item to check off of your "to do" list?
- Do you spend quality time in prayer with the Lord? Are you guilty of offering God microwave prayers?

We have all been guilty at some time or another. We get so busy that we neglect to put first things first. This creates an open door for sin and destruction. Consider the story of Cain and Abel. Cain was guilty of presenting God leftovers. His lack of understanding of presenting God with the first led to envy and jealousy that resulted in the murder of his brother. Let us learn from the lesson that Cain so easily failed. We must sweep away the sin and destruction that lies in wait from our doors. God is waiting to receive us. All we have to do is STOP what we are doing and begin to do well.

When it was time for the harvest, Cain presented some of his crops as a gift to the Lord. Abel also brought a gift—the best of the firstborn lambs from his flock. The Lord accepted Abel and his gift, but he did not accept Cain and his gift. This made Cain very angry, and he looked dejected. "Why are you so angry?" the Lord asked Cain. "Why do you look so dejected? You will be accepted if you do what is right. But if you refuse to do what is right, then watch out! Sin is crouching at the door, eager to control you. But you must subdue it and be its master."
Genesis 4:3-7 NLT

Chapter 6

It's Not What I Thought it Was

Throughout different stages in our lives we have a vivid vision of what our lives will be. As a little girl, I envisioned living in a big mansion spending my days enjoying a life of leisure with a rich, handsome husband, wonderful children and people who were employed for the sole purpose of making my life carefree. My dream came right from the movies that I watched as a child where Doris Day and a cast of others lived happily ever after. Even now, just the thought brings a smile to my face. As we grow older, though our dream may be slightly altered by the reality of our experiences, deep inside we still hold on to our "perfect world" expectations for life. That's called hope.

I remember when the Lord called me to ministry. I had this glorious vision of standing before thousands ministering the Word as people received salvation and forever changing their lives. The Lord has used me in ministry, however, not quite as I had imagined in my mind. Instead it has been one life at a time in some of the most peculiar places and forums you can imagine. There have been times I have tried to hide that call, however it always reveals itself when I speak.

I still hold on to the vision I had so vividly created in my imagination. And though I am much wiser now, I cherish the vision because it is the catalyst of my faith and hope for being used in the ministry of God. It keeps me focused on seeking God for his will and direction. I've learned that the vision is not always what I think it is, but it is what it has been ordained to be. I understand that God's ways and thoughts are very different from mine.

For my thoughts are not your thoughts, neither are your ways my way. For as the heavens are higher than the earth, so are my ways higher than your ways and my thoughts than your thoughts.
Isaiah 55:8-9 KJV

Chapter 7

Help I've Fallen and I Can't Get Up

Anyone who was born in the sixties may remember the commercial of the elderly lady lying in the floor screaming these words: "Help I've fallen and I can't get up." It was an advertisement for some sort of medical alert device. I don't remember the product, but I do, after all of the years that have gone by, remember the exact statement that was used to market that product. I had no idea at that time that I would utter those exact words so many times in my journey with Christ.

Frequently falling is depicted as backsliding or walking away from Christ. While this may be true, the scope of "fallen" is much broader. You can be saved and love the Lord and be in a fallen state. If you have been saved for an extended period of years, chances are that you have had this experience. This is such a hard and lonely place. It is a place where you can see everything that is wrong but can't quite figure out how to get out and stay out. It is like being at the bottom of a big hole and looking up at the top. You can see the way out but don't have the power or ability to get out. You run up that very steep incline again and again, just a few steps from freedom and then slide right down that slope back to the very place you are trying to escape.

Somewhere deep within you hold fast to hope. You can see the destination, but struggle to get back on track. This is not a place that we enjoy being in, but it is a necessary part of the journey. This is a place that forces you to be transparent before the Lord. In this place you are prime to be re-made and molded by the Lord. If you have ever been in this fallen place, you know that this is a place where you have very real and frank discussions with the Lord. Desperate situations sometimes call for impractical reactions. You drop the "thee" and "thou" along with the other things religious rituals have taught you about prayer. You know that you can't stay where you are and that if the Lord does not rescue you, you will go over the edge. You have tried everything you know to do. Full of desperation and despair in this destitute place, you cry out, "Lord help me! I have fallen and I can't get up!" You recognize that deliverance will only come through the merciful hand of God.

God loves you. You are the recipient of his grace and mercy daily. He is waiting for your call. He is there to rescue you. He will destroy the chains that are restraining you from the life he has intended for you.

Listen! The Lord's arm is not too weak to save you, nor is his ear too deaf to hear your call.
Isaiah 59:1 NLT

Chapter 8

Identity Crisis

I have spent most of my adult life being who I thought I was supposed to be through the eyes of others. In the church it was a great woman of God. In the business world, it was the senior manager that delivers on time, every time with a solution to every problem since the beginning of time. As a wife and mother it was a rock, the tower of strength that finds a way to take care of everything, never faltering with absolute zero weakness in times when strength is required. I could go on, but that is more than enough for any one person to live up to. In the midst of being who everyone else needs me to be, who am I really?

There are times that I stop and wonder who is this person I call me. I know fragments of who I am, but I can't recall ever having the complete liberty to just be me. As far as I can remember, I have filled a role to meet the needs of other people. There are times I experience an inner struggle wanting to just be human and even weak. Sometimes I want to admit to the world that I don't have all the answers. I long to let go of every emotion that has been imprisoned within me but can't because I am too busy being what everyone else in my life needs.

So who am I really? Well, it's whoever I need to be at that particular time. For isn't that who God is? He is multi-faceted. For the sick he is a healer, for the broken he is a restorer, for the hungry he is a provider and for the lost he is a savior. I am the offspring of God. I am created in his image. I look like and, most of the time, act like my father. I demonstrate my father's attributes by extending myself to others, often in the absence of appreciation or fulfillment.

In those quiet moments when the day is done, I am simply Daddy's little girl seeking comfort in the wisdom of his word and the generosity of his grace. I know that tomorrow I will once again be who God says that I am.

So God created man in his own image. In the image of God created him, male and female created he them.
Genesis 1:27 KJV

Chapter 9

Lord I Need a Do-Over

How many times have you run back to the Lord needing a do-over? How frequently have you had to return to square one to try to get it right? I attended a business seminar where the top producer in this multi-million dollar company was the keynote speaker. I anxiously sat on the edge of my seat awaiting the pearls of wisdom that would be spoken from the lips of this very successful and wealthy entrepreneur. He had already mastered this business that I had been recently introduced to. My excitement was heightened because the speaker was a spirit-filled believer and openly acknowledged God as key to his achievement. I sat eagerly with pen and pad in hand ready to take the most copious notes. His advice was short but profound. "Follow the pattern. Don't try and create anything new. It's already been done. Just follow the pattern." He went on to say that ninety-five percent of the people in the room would not listen and would try to recreate the wheel.

Sound familiar? We've always been taught that we have to go where there is no path and leave a trail behind us. After all, isn't that the mark of greatness? Very few have told us about the wisdom in following the trail that has already been made before us. Interestingly, it is the same with the Word of God, God's covenant for our lives. We have wasted years trying to recreate and redefine the Word of God. Today, we will reset the course of our journey to move towards God's purpose for our lives. The path is narrow and straight. We will follow the trail that Jesus has left for us.

We will mimic our Father. We will walk, talk, think and act like our Father. We will transition from servant-hood to son-ship in our Lord and Savior, Jesus Christ. God has called us to be sons and daughters. Sons and daughters are joint owners and heirs. Servants are hired hands. Stop and think about it. Do you want the privileges of being a son or daughter or the privilege of being a servant? When was the last time you saw a servant climb up in the lap of the Father? Let's look at this a little further. Think about the roles in various relationships: mother-child, father-son, employer-employee, and master-servant. Though being a servant in the kingdom of God is a great honor, it is an even greater honor to be considered a child of the king.

We have a need to better understand our covenant with God. A covenant is a legally binding contract; it is an agreement between two or more parties. Covenants require quid-pro-quo clauses. The covenant defines the requirements of all parties that are bound by the contract. The parties agree to fulfill the stipulations defined in the contract.

Our covenant with the Lord was established at the cross. The agreement has not been revised. It remains the same. The Lord continues to honor and uphold the contract. In fact, when the contract has been breached, it is because we are the ones who fail to meet our promises outlined in the agreement. We fail time and time again in honoring our covenant with God. We want to pick and choose the parts of the covenant that we want to honor. Yet, we expect God to fulfill his commitment word for word and within the context of our imaginations and self-made timelines.

There are consequences for breaching a contract. It will always cost you something. In the Old Testament, the penalty for breaching a covenant was death. Guess what? It has not changed. Have you ever heard the phrase, "dead man walking?" When Adam ate from the forbidden fruit, he experienced a spiritual separation from God. He experienced a spiritual death. You can be dead in your relationships, marriage, peace, joy, finances, health, and even dead in your thinking. Shall I go on? I didn't think so. You get the picture. How merciful is our Father to his children. He is giving us a do-over and it starts today. Follow the path that Christ has left for us and you will be certain to reach your destination.

If you are willing and obedient, you shall eat the good of the land; but if you refuse and rebel, you shall be eaten by the sword; for the mouth of the Lord has spoken.
Isaiah 1:19-20 ESV

Chapter 10

Just Like a Hamster on a Wheel

At the beginning of every year, I like many, reflect on the previous year as I think about the goals that I will set for the New Year. As I reflected on the previous twelve months, I realized that not just the last year, but also several years before, I had not completely achieved the major goals I had wanted to accomplish. This prompted me to consider all of the things I was involved in. I needed to really understand where I was investing my time.

I have always taken pride in participating in activities that contributed to my personal development and advancement of my family. I wrote down each and every initiative that was drawing from my time. The initial list had about thirty or so items. I was involved in business networks, distribution of wellness products and real estate. I reviewed each of these activities with a keen and critical eye. I found that these activities were good endeavors but were not necessarily good for me to participate in at that time. As I reflected over the prior years, I concluded that I had a lot of activity that was not producing results commensurate with the time being invested. There was little return on investment. Simply stated, the time I spent doing 'good' things did not produce the desired results.

To further exasperate matters, the quality of relationship with the Lord and my family was diminished because my time was being absorbed in other areas. Everything that I have ever committed my energy to has been for the benefit of my family, which I realized was being tossed to the side and neglected.

I was deeply saddened as I looked at that list. The Lord spoke to me and instructed that I should discontinue everything on the list that I did not absolutely have to do. I checked off each activity that I could discontinue. I did just that. I simply stopped. I inactivated my real estate license. I withdrew from the networking groups. I not only stopped but gave away all of my collateral for my wellness business.

I focused on the items that I needed to do but for whatever reason had not completed. I set timelines and began to take the required actions to successfully complete the items that remained on my list.

Interestingly, what remained on the list are the things that are most important, my relationship with God, my family and my overall health. Things stopped spinning out of control when I jumped off of the hamster wheel.

Are you on a hamster wheel? Are you running with all of your might and still in the same place? I encourage you to stop and take a moment to reflect upon where you have been. Re-examine your priorities. Make sure that your priorities are aligned with the things that are most important in your life. Life is a lot more fulfilling when we step off the hamster wheel that has a final destination of nowhere.

Come unto me, all ye that labor and are heavy laden, and I will give you rest.
Matthew 11:28 KJV

Chapter

11

Holier Than Thou

Have you ever been called or thought someone was holier than thou? What exactly does that mean? This term is used very loosely, typically to describe someone that has been deemed to be a super saint or super spiritual. Let's really think about this for a moment. We haphazardly criticize someone that is in pursuit of God. We make them feel bad for seeking to be like the Lord. We rarely stop and consider that we are criticizing the very thing that the Lord requires. The scriptures teach us that without holiness no man shall see God.

When you look at it from this perspective, it may just cause us to stop and repent. We live in a society that accepts and embraces any and everything, except holiness. I was recently in a discussion and was called "holier than thou" because my viewpoint was different than the party I was speaking with. It wasn't until later the next day that I realized it was a compliment. You see God is my Father. He is a holy God. I was created in his image. I look like him and I portray his characteristics.

When someone calls you "holier than thou," just smile and tell them thank you. They are simply saying, "You act just like your daddy." That, my friend, is an extreme compliment. Don't let anyone discourage you in your pursuit of God. Holiness is a sign that you are drawing near to God.

For I am the Lord your God; ye shall therefore sanctify yourselves and ye shall be Holy for I am Holy.
Leviticus 11:44

Chapter 12

White Noise

We all have white noise that surrounds us from time to time. Sometimes the sound of the noise is louder than normal. White noise by definition is noise that contains many frequencies with equal intensities. In Christian ease, white noise can be defined as distractors. Distractors are things that absorb your attention and drain you of your strength emotionally and physically.

A few examples of white noise are stressful work environments, strained relationships, health scares and even financial challenges. White noise is designed to frustrate you and cause you to lose focus. It comes to derail you in your pursuit of God, your dreams and your goals. White noise is intense. If allowed, it will overtake you and even drown out the voice of God.

To overcome white noise, you must recognize that it is just noise. You must understand what it is designed to do and make the necessary adjustment to silence the noise. You may not be able to immediately get rid of it, but you can surely mute it.

When dealing with white noise, it is important to recognize the things you can affect. Get a plan of action. Make sure you understand the source of the noise. This will help you quickly put it into perspective. This alone will lower the frequency of the noise. Finally, keep your mind focused on your priorities and not the white noise.

I suggest directing your thoughts to praising God. Hum your favorite hymn or worship song. It drowns out the white noise. God gives you direction and strategies in the midst of the noise. Before you know it the noise is silenced. It has failed in defeating you. You are at peace. You have regained balance and control in your life. You are victorious in silencing the noise.

And he arose, and rebuked the wind and said unto the sea, "Peace be still." And the wind ceased and there was a great calm.
Mark 4:39 KJV

Chapter 13

Stop Back Seat Driving

How often do you have to remind yourself that God is in control? One of my favorite scriptures is, "Being confident of this very thing, that he which hath begun a good work in you will perform it until the day of Jesus Christ" (Philippians 1:6 KJV). We have a tendency to want to control everything concerning our lives. It is difficult to be a passenger. We want to drive and map out the course. We have to be reminded, the steps of a good man (or woman) are ordered by the Lord.

Most things we try to control lead to being out of control. This results in making emotional or less than optimal decisions. Making a good decision does not automatically mean it is the best decision. We find ourselves in the permissive, rather than the perfect will of God. Being in the permissive will of God can lead to unnecessary detours that delay our arrival to the destination that God has preordained for us.

There are several types of back seat drivers. There are over achievers that go after things with gusto. Over achievers are the people that take a basic idea or concept and quickly forge ahead to make it happen their way and then call it God. There are the planners. God gives them a word and they plot out step-by-step how things will happen. Planners sometimes have difficulty with execution and often get stuck in the planning mode. There are the directors. Directors have the plan down to the utmost detail. Directors like to instruct other people, including God, in the what, how and when to perform their assignment to manifest their vision. There are the dreamers. Dreamers sit idly by holding on to the dream. Dreamers can miss the voice and direction of God while waiting for the promise of God to magically appear. Finally, there are the naysayers. Naysayers are the people who absolutely refuse to move from where they are. This group is comprised of four types of people:

1) Those that fear rejection,
2) Those that fear failure,
3) Those who fear the unknown, and
4) Those who are comfortable with the status quo, preferring to hold on to the past instead of embracing the present and reaching for the future.

Which are you? We vacillate between them. I know I have.

There is a lesson that we can learn from our pets. I have a Scottish terrier named Prince. When I pick up my keys and tell him "let's go," he runs to the car door. When I open the door he jumps in on the driver side and immediately moves to the passenger side. He will stand up and look out the window. Occasionally, I will open the window and he will stick his head out and enjoy the breeze. He sits in that passenger seat looking over at me with such contentment, happy to be on the journey, happy to be in my presence, not knowing exactly where we are going but trusting me to get us there.

I am certainly not advocating that we act like dogs. I am advocating that we are mindful in remembering that we are sheep. Sheep are docile animals that can be led by a staff. They are vulnerable and are protected by the shepherd. The shepherd takes his sheep to green pastures. This is the place of safety, food, water and rest. Some might say that sheep are dumb. I would argue that sheep are one of the wisest animals ever created. Jesus taught us about sheep in one of his many parables:

> *To him the gatekeeper opens. The sheep hear his voice and he calls his own sheep by name, and leads them out. When*

he has brought out all his own, he goes before them and the sheep follow him, for they know his voice. A stranger they will not follow...
John 10:3-4 ESV

Chapter 14

Five Minutes of Praise

Chances are that unless you are in full-time ministry your time spent before the Lord has been derailed from time to time. Go ahead, be honest, how many times have you committed yourself to pray or read the Word for one hour daily? How often have you planned to get up every morning and pray for an hour before leaving for work? I will be the first to confess my guilt. Almost every time I have tried to structure my life, my best intentions have been derailed. Every time I failed, I repeatedly attempted to get it back on track.

Then one day it happened. I was assessing my progress as to where I was in achieving the three goals I had set for my life. I realized that I continued to do the same "good" things that caused me to fail repeatedly. One of my goals was spiritual growth. I wanted to be closer to God. I had a goal to pray and read the word of God daily for a specified period of time. As I assessed my spiritual goal, I found myself viewing this goal with a microscopic eye to really understand exactly what spiritual growth meant. I discovered that I had activities that I had categorized as spiritual but had failed to take the time to define what spirituality meant to me. I didn't have a point of reference to measure whether or not I had achieved this goal. As I dissected this goal, I realized that I continued to fail because my goal was not representative of what I wanted to achieve. I had to redefine this goal. The goal I really wanted to achieve was a Bible based relationship with the Lord. The Bible defined the guidelines. Relationship was the goal. I wanted a relationship with the Lord that is governed according to the Word of God.

Now that I had a good understanding of the goal and my desired outcome, I began to think about relationships and how they come about. Association with someone in various intervals for extended periods of time forms relationships. The nature of the relationship is generally determined by what each party is willing to invest of themselves. There are various types of relationships. For example, the relationship you have in a marriage with a spouse is very different that you would experience with a work colleague or repairman. The type of relationship that I want with the Lord supersedes marriage. I want to be his adoring daughter, showered by the wisdom and love of her doting father.

As I took stock of my misfires and failures, I gave serious consideration to what I could really commit to and successfully achieve. I thought five minutes. I can commit to telling God thank you for five minutes everyday.

Five minutes changed my life. Five minutes changed my world, my family, my job, my finances and my health. Five minutes led me into God's perfect will for my life. Five minutes led me into communion with the God. Five minutes have turned into hours. An interesting outcome is that I always have time to accomplish those busy tasks that seemed to crowd my life. Five minutes anchored me. The investment of those five minutes has yielded peace, direction, victory and success. God has been attentive to the smallest of my petitions. Five minutes spent with the Lord can accomplish more than you will in a lifetime.

Will you commit to spending five minutes a day with the Lord? It will not only change your life, it will also change the life of those that you love as well.

Praise ye the Lord. O give thanks unto the Lord, for he is good and his mercy endures forever.
Psalm 106:1 KJV

Chapter 15

When My Mind Is Fixed on Jesus

Scripture teaches us that as a man thinks, so is he. Deep, right? Not really, let's review it in the simplest of terms. What you think about the most is what you become. Anything I have ever achieved started with a thought and became a relentless pursuit. I thought about it continuously. I read books on it. I studied it. I researched the Internet. I committed what I learned to memory. I formed habits. I practiced it until it became part of who I am.

King David was a worshipper. In the midst of his self-created pitfalls he was a worshipper. He is found continually adoring God throughout the scriptures. In Psalms 34, he decrees that he will bless the Lord at all times declaring that God's praise would continually be in his mouth. When your thoughts become who you are, what you pursue becomes second nature. It is part of your conscious and subconscious. It easily governs your actions.

Like King David, when my mind is fixed on Jesus, my thoughts and actions are on autopilot. I easily take on the character and mindset of our Lord. I self correct my actions.

Let me give you another example. Have you ever climbed or observed someone climb the corporate career ladder? Their focus is on attaining the desired position. Activities and actions are aligned with attaining the goal. This includes obtaining training, being politically correct and positioning themselves with people that can assist in attaining promotion to the next level. They become a company cheerleader. Too frequently they leave collateral damage in their path, long before they attain their goal. Their thinking transforms them into who they are trying to become. Does that describe you or someone you know?

I've been there and done that. It is a place of instability with an indescribable price to be paid. There are those that know exactly what I am referring to. In fact, this may be what you are going through right now. However, there are those of you that have experienced challenges, successes and defeats that have prompted you to reorder your priorities. You redirected your affections back to Jesus, realizing that when your mind is fixed on Jesus it changes your perspective in life. You become sure and effective.

Be encouraged today. Just consider some of the by products of having your mind fixed on Jesus.

- The angel of the Lord is assigned to you as your bodyguard. Psalm 34:7
- You know the Lord is good and because you trust him you are blessed. Psalm 34:8
- Because you are his, you don't want for anything. Psalm 34:9
- You pursue God and he does not withhold any good thing from you. Psalm 34:10
- You learn to watch what you say and whom you say it about. Psalm 34:13
- You pursue peace. You choose not to get caught up in games or politics. Psalm 34:15
- You still have challenges, battles and life issues, but God gives you peace and direction that brings deliverance. Psalm 34:19
- God controls your destiny. You go through trials, but you always come out whole. Psalm 34:20
- God has your back. He intervenes on your behalf at just the right moment. He has the final say over your situation and your life. Trusting God pays high yield dividends. Psalm 34:22

Wow, just thinking about these benefits leaves me speechless. I wonder what you will be thinking about today, this week and the rest of your life. As for me, my mind is fixed on Jesus.

I will bless the Lord at all times. His praise shall continually be in my mouth.
Psalm 34:1 KJV

Chapter 16

Seeking Him Early

The majority of Christians have been taught, and rightfully so, to give God the first portion of their day. For most this seems like a no brainer. In a previous chapter, I shared with you how five minutes transformed my life. I didn't realize the importance of the timing of those five minutes. One morning I slept until six-thirty, two hours after the normal time I usually get up. I arose and started my day with the Lord. I set the coffee pot to brew and proceeded to my special place where I have my morning coffee with the Lord. About twenty to thirty minutes later I noticed something was quite different. I could hear the noises of the rumblings of life. I heard cars, school buses and the hustle and bustle of my neighbors starting their day. I was distracted by the sounds of life around me.

Something was different. Something was missing. It occurred to me that I am up every morning at four-thirty. At four-thirty in the morning it is quiet. The neighbors are not scurrying through the neighborhood and the children are still asleep. I realized the peace, solitude and the specialness of stealing away to Jesus before the breaking of day. That four-thirty hour for me is an intimate interlude with my Lord and Savior. It is when we sit quietly. It is the special time that my father sets aside just for me. I truly get to be Daddy's girl in the wee hours of the morning. Without fail, he gives me direction for my day and my life. I didn't realize just how important the hour was. Well, today is Saturday and I am having my morning coffee with the Lord. It is four-thirty in the morning.

O God, You are my God, early will I seek thee. My soul thirsts for you, my flesh longs for you in a dry thirsty land where there is no water.
Psalm 63:1 NKJV

Chapter

17

Put It on the Line

We have transformed every part of our lives to be politically and socially correct. We have permitted corporations, schools, politics and media to strip us of our beliefs and convictions. We have willingly submitted to framing our worldview into nicely packaged words that don't offend or cause any discomfort to the listener. What about the discomfort it causes you? We exercise great caution because every word spoken brings unwanted scrutiny and sometimes retribution. This is especially true for those that are in the media spot light.

Expressing a differing opinion does not have to be rude, hateful or hurtful. We carefully craft our words to ensure we are not ill perceived by others. We expend energy to ensure that we are socially acceptable, losing the value that our words can have in building and strengthening people and relationships. We conform to what is deemed an acceptable norm but is in deep contrast to our beliefs. We enslave the pureness of our thoughts to the script that society writes for each of us. We conform to the world allowing our voice to be silenced. Who are you anyway?

What if Jesus pretended to be someone he was not in order to avoid offending others? What if he spent his time telling people what was comfortable for them to hear and not the truth that brought forth deliverance and healing? Can you imagine what would have happened if the woman he compared to a dog became offended? Can you imagine how uncomfortable the blind man was when Jesus rubbed spit into his eyes?

We suppress our true opinions in fear of losing our jobs, popularity, being ridiculed and even becoming a social outcast. We are accountable for people we could have helped, but failed to because we didn't want to risk being offensive. We choose to speak what is expected from us rather than what we really think. After all, it is not wise to rock the boat by having a non-conforming point of view.

We observe leaders doing things that are morally and ethically wrong and turn our heads to protect our personal interest. We are fearful of losing those six and seven figure incomes. We have placed a price tag on our own ethics and integrity.

There will come a time in which you will have to put it on line. God did not create us to be bobble-heads. Philippians 2:5 encourage us to have the mind of Christ. Christ did not turn his head or hold his tongue when he destroyed the businesses of the many vendors who had made the temple a retail outlet. I can imagine the reaction of the disciples when Christ told the woman that it was not appropriate to give the children's bread to dogs. Her ability to accept the unadulterated truth resulted in her petition being granted. Her daughter was healed.

Think about the times you have not been completely forthright in sharing your thoughts. How often have you said, Happy Holidays instead of Merry Christmas? How much time do you spend selecting Christmas cards that say nothing about Christmas? How many times have you agreed with a boss for fear of losing your job? Have there been times you should have spoken up but chose to sit in silence? Have you done something that was in contrast to your ethics and integrity to maintain social acceptance?

In some form or fashion we have all made compromises that have placed price tags upon our personal beliefs. I made the decision to take the risk of being forthright with my opinions and thoughts. I have watched too many people be hurt because people who were in a position that gave them a voice refused to speak out. They were unwilling to risk their personal interest to make a difference in the lives of others. I made the conscious choice to put it on the line. I choose to tell leaders and executives the truth without the craftily constructed words. I am respectful and I am honest. I realize that there were only two things that can be taken from me: 1) employment, and 2) whatever else I am willing to give up.

A job can end at any moment. Silence and agreement does not guarantee job security. It is called "at will" employment. "At will" means that the employer or employee can end employment at any time. The only restriction is the termination must not violate state or federal law.

What you give of yourself is far more valuable than a job. Character, ethics, values and morality cannot be taken unless it is given away. That part of me is not for sale. I am willing to pay the price to keep them because they are priceless.

Being candid and honest with executives began a healing process in the company where I work. Leaders are taking stock of themselves. Transparency in communications and actions are improving the work lives of employees. Trust is being restored as people lay down the masks they have hidden behind. As expected, for some it is more difficult than others. I have the peace that comes with knowing that I have done what has been required of me. One man will plant, another man will water, but it is always God who brings the increase.

One final thought: it's okay for you to say Merry Christmas. You'll be surprised at how many people will be delighted to hear it because it is really what was in their heart to say, but they did not want to offend you. Believe it or not, we have unwittingly served two masters in our quest for social correctness; no man can serve two masters, you will hate one and love the other. Who are you serving?

And if it seem evil unto you to serve the Lord, choose you this day whom ye will serve; whether the gods which your fathers served that were on the other side of the flood, or the gods of the Amorites, in whose land ye dwell; but as for me and my house, we will serve the Lord.
Joshua 24:15 KJV

Chapter 18

How Do You See Him?

Jesus asked his disciples, "Who do people say that the Son of Man is?" (Matthew 6:13 ESV) The responses varied, but all had one common thread; they were all from the vantage point of the limitations of the minds of man as to how they saw him. We have spent our lives listening to the viewpoint of who man has said that Jesus is, but we all must answer the same question that Jesus asked the of Peter, "But who do you say that I am?" (Matthew 6:15 ESV)

This poses the question, how do you really see Him? Is he a baby that is wrapped in rags in a manger? Is he just a carpenter? Are you among those that would contend he is just a great philosopher? Is he a mere myth or fable whose story has been told throughout many generations? Is he your genie whose purpose is to fulfill your every command?

How you see him determines who he is in your life. Let's consider Jesus, the baby in a manger. For as long as I have lived, I have celebrated being a year older on my birthday, yet every Christmas, several thousand years later, we continue to put King Jesus right back in that manger reducing him to an infant state. Infants are powerless; they have to be cared for and nurtured. Sadly, every time we make him the baby Jesus, we reduce his power in our life.

How do you really see him? Is your relationship with him so casual and familiar that you see him as your equal? What place have you given him in your life? Do you even recognize when he comes in the room? Have you restricted him to your religious traditions and ideals?

I challenge you to change your perspective. Open your heart and enlighten your mind and spirit. Who do I say that he is? The most I can ever imagine is the least he will ever be. He is a holy savior, a sovereign king and master of the universe. He is to be reverenced, worshipped and adored. He is the son of the only true and infinitely wise God. He is everything to me. How do you see him?

Is not this the carpenter's son? Is not his mother called Mary? And his brethren James and Joses and Simon and Judas? And his sisters, are they not all with us? Whence then hath this man all these things? And they were offended in him. But

Jesus said unto them, a prophet is not without honor save in his own country and in his own house. And he did not many mighty works there because of their unbelief.

Matthew 13:55-58

Chapter 19

Just Do It

"Just do it" is a phrase that was made popular through the Nike shoe commercials. What does this mean? What is the empowering message behind those three little words that consist of only eight letters? "Just Do It" implies that one knows what to do or at least has thought about doing something.

Perhaps it is a dream, career change or life long goal. What is your just do it? As I thought about this vision-provoking phrase, my thoughts reverted to the self-imposed handicaps that stifle dreams and goals. These handicaps are the simple things that we "just don't do."

To really illuminate the simplicity of "just do it," it should be restated to say "NO MORE EXCUSES." Yes, no more self-induced reasons to fail. No more excuses for not obtaining victory. If we expect to achieve greatness, we must conquer the basic battles in our daily lives. These battles represent basic training that prepares us to be victorious in greater challenges. To successfully complete basic training, we must attain consistency, discipline, perseverance, and measureable success in the very rudimentary trials in life.

This sounds relatively easy, however, we find ourselves constantly struggling to attain success in these areas. Lets look at some examples of areas where we repeatedly fall short:

- Proper diet and nutrition. How many times have you promised yourself that you were going to start tomorrow or after the holidays?
- Responsible finance management. What was your biggest emotional purchase? Are you buying your wants and begging for your needs? Are you just a pass through for your paycheck? Does it pass through your hand directly to a creditor?
- Business. How many times have you thought about starting a business and never take any action beyond the thought?
- Is there a book waiting to be written by you? Don't know where to start? Just start. Pick up the pen and write.

This is just a short list. What dreams and goals do you have laying dormant in your life? How many tomorrow's are you waiting for? Start today. It's time to stop making excuses. It's time to accomplish your dreams and goals. Start by completing your basic training. Create a plan. Make sure you set a timeline and define how you will measure success. This becomes the foundation that will catapult you into achieving your dreams and goals. Before you know it, you will have gone from "just doing it" to "JUST DONE IT."

I can do all things through Christ who strengthens me.
Philippians 4:13 NKJV

Chapter 20

Hast Thou Considered My Servant?

You never know what you are truly made of until you have been tested to the extreme. Sometimes we go though seasons in our lives where there is one tragedy or seemingly insurmountable challenge after another. When you think you have reached your breaking point, something else happens. Consider the losses and trials you have experienced over the years. And yet, you are still standing. You are still holding it together. You continue to navigate the path of life, day after day.

Like Job, many of us have had to face the one thing that we have feared the most; the thing that we were certain we could not survive; yet we did. Oh sure, we probably did not get an A+, but most importantly, we passed the course. Do you remember how that one trial, coupled with so many other disruptions, changed your character? Your perspective changed. You approach challenges differently. Certain things no longer upset you. You maintain your composure and resolve. You are purposefully selective in choosing where to invest your valuable time and energy. You simply deal with the challenges as they come. As painful and agonizing as the trial was, it was all a part of the refining process to become who God predestined you to be.

You would not be who you are today without the experiences from yesterday. Sometimes God volunteers you for certain trials to expedite the process that leads you to your destiny. There are three things you should always remember:

    1) God sets limits.
    2) He is always in control, and
    3) He already knows your outcome.

Prior to Job's greatest trial, he practiced religion. Job practiced what had been taught by generations before him. He prayed "just in case" prayers for his children. Life was good. Job's world was perfect. Sound familiar? God employed Satan to frustrate Job, to rob him of his prized possessions that also included the people he loved. I am certain this trial felt like an eternity to Job. It was during this extended season that Job transitioned from religion to having a relationship with God. Job discovered things about himself that he would have never known had it not been for the trial he successfully endured. He suffered loss, betrayal, illness and humiliation.

Astonishingly, the faith that had been instilled in him withstood every test, even when he wanted to close his eyes and die. It was in this trial that Job gained the revelation of his own frailty, weakness and insignificance. He saw God. Job spoke with clarity when he said, "I have heard of thee by the hearing of the ear; but now my eye sees you." (Job 4:25 NKJV).

We must all be tested and pass the test. The end reward is to see the God who has redeemed us. In trials we discover the very depth of our faith. God reveals himself to us that we may know him. If you are in the midst of a trial that you never imagined you would be able to survive, it may just be that God has asked Satan, "Have you considered my servant...."

And he (Nebuchadnezzar) commanded the certain mighty men that were in his army to bind Shadrach, Meshach and Abed-nego, and to cast them into the burning fiery furnace. Then these men were bound in their coats, their trousers, and their turbans, and their other garments and were cast into the midst of the burning fiery furnace. Therefore because the king's commandment was urgent, and the furnace was exceeding hot, the flame of the fire killed those men that took up Shadrach, Meshach, and Abed-nego. And these three men, Shadrach, Meshach, and Abed-nego, fell down bound into the

midst of the burning fiery furnace. Then King Nebuchadnezzar was astonished, and rose up in haste, and spoke, and said unto his counselors, did not we cast three men bound into the midst of the fire? They answered and said unto the king, "True, O king." "Look!" he answered, "I see four men loose, walking in the midst of the fire, and they are not hurt, and the form of the fourth is like the Son of God."
Daniel 3: 20 – 25 NKJV

Chapter 21

Because You Fought

From time to time, we find ourselves in the midst of a battle that weighs heavily on our hearts. Without hesitation, we pray, fast and wage spiritual warfare on behalf of our loved ones and friends. It is easy to fight for someone that we care for. It is a bit more difficult when you are fighting for you. My pastor once said, "The things we fail the most at are things that require something from us." This is a statement that is worthy of consideration.

I am one of those people that set goals and timelines to accomplish things that are important to me. I have set and achieved education, career and income goals. I create task lists to accomplish the tedious items that can sometimes be overwhelming when life spins out of control.

I find it intriguing that I easily achieve every goal that is external, but struggle with goals that can only be accomplished within me. It is easy to enroll in an education program that has defined requirements and timelines for successful completion. Income and career goals can be accomplished with hard work and good business relationships.

Then there are the goals that require something more of you, such as nutrition and weight management. Like most people, I have tried lots of different things and have had some success. However, I haven't reached that tipping point that produces sustained life altering success. One thing that is certain, I have learned exactly what I must do to achieve my goal. I just don't want to do it. It requires something of me. Amazing, right? I know exactly what I must do to reach my goal. I even know how to do it. Time and time again, I have made counter-productive decisions. I consciously made the decision not to be victorious. When we know what to do and choose not to do it, we choose failure as our outcome. Yes, failure is an option. We have the option to fail or be successful.

Do you have a dream that is simmering on the back burner? Is there something that you know you should be doing, but are just not doing it? What is required of you? You are worth fighting for. Let us agree today that we will commit to fulfilling what is required of us to become victorious.

I have fought a good fight, I have finished my course, I have kept the faith.
2Timothy 4:7 KJV

Chapter 22

Time Is Running Out

Have you ever watched sand in an hourglass drift steadily downward from the upper to the lower chamber until it has emptied? This is a depiction of our life. The time seems to drift away slowly. Towards the end it seems to slip away more rapidly. We all have a designated hour to die. I, like a lot of people, haven't really considered the hour of death beyond salvation in Christ Jesus. I always imagined, or should I say assumed, that I would be an old lady who had accomplished everything that I had ever imagined doing in my life.

I naively assumed that there was no way I could die until I fulfilled God's purpose for my life. That sounds nice, holy and even reasonable. Until recently, I never considered that God would use me to start a work and use someone else to finish it. Even more sobering is that it is even possible that I may not live to see it. The Apostle Paul said, "I have planted, Apollos watered, but God gave the increase" (1 Corinthians 3:6 KJV). We assume that when we start something we will be there through completion of the work. We all want to see the end result of our labor. However, it may not be the will of God for your life.

My sister, Toni, loved God and was fulfilling God's plan for her life. She was excited about what the Lord was doing. The Lord had gifted her with an incredible love for children. Toni owned a day care and was in the midst of expanding to accommodate more children. She had the passion you have when God has anointed you and given you a clear vision to accomplish the work he has assigned to you. Toni was walking in purpose while watching the plan of God being manifested in her life. She was a few week's away from fulfilling her destiny. Suddenly, she died. She was fifty-six years old. There were no known health issues. She did not feel well that day and died later that evening at home.

Toni's vision will be fulfilled. Her pastor committed to open the childcare facility. It will bear the name and legacy that Toni began, "Auntie Toni's Day Care."

I learned several truths through this very painful experience. One of the most important lessons is regarding life. We must participate in life to its fullest. We must do everything that we can towards fulfilling our part in God's master plan. The sand in our individual hourglasses is drifting downward with time. As it reaches the end, it is certain that it will slip away until it is no more. Jesus said:

> *"I must work the works of him that sent me, while it is day: the night is coming when no one can work."*
> *John 9:4 NKJV*

Chapter 23

After the Storm

We have experienced many storms in our lifetime. The Tsunami in Japan and Hurricane Katrina in Louisiana are most notable in the last few years. The lives lost during these disasters were monumental. Even today, there are people that have not been found and are presumed deceased. We still mourn the deaths of those that were lost during these natural disasters.

The media coverage heightens our awareness to the reality of the horror of the storm as we watch the reports unfold on our televisions. Survivors are interviewed. The newscaster reports on historical comparisons, providing images of death to help the viewer better understand the magnitude of the devastation. Over the next several days and sometimes weeks, the newsreels are replayed repeatedly recasting the images as the damage and losses are assessed.

We marvel at the display of hope and courage of the survivors as they pick up the broken pieces and plan their future.

Through the loss of loved ones, friends, homes and businesses inner strength is birthed. The survivors have an overwhelming sense of survival and determination to rise above the devastation that has been wrought in their lives. They have been shaken but not uprooted. The source of their strength is still connected.

There are storms that don't get the attention of the media. No one even knows that they have occurred except the person who has experienced it. There are storms in which we suffer a devastating loss such as a parent, spouse, sibling, child or close friend. There are some losses that we can accept more easily and be at peace. Others hit us like a Tsunami. There is no comfort. There is no peace. There is absolutely no understanding. Even though you know that God is present, you feel shaken to the very core of your being. You are not angry with God, but you are angry and broken-hearted. You don't know what to pray or even say to God. You know that he is still present in the midst of your pain. You do the only thing you know to do. You just keep moving forward in the midst of the debris and destruction that is left behind from the tragedy you have experienced. As you walk through the pain, you quietly wait for a word from the Lord to help you make sense of it all.

This is a place where our awareness is heightened to the true sovereignty of God. We have sung about his sovereignty in our hymns. We have proclaimed it in our testimonies that fit neatly into the context of our picture perfect worldview. It is in this valley we obtain a very real understanding that God's thoughts and ways don't fit into the neat little box of how we have framed our world.

God does not explain himself to us. In fact, it doesn't matter if we understand. It is in this glimpse of his sovereignty that you become acutely aware that you are not in control. God does not need your approval or consent. You have a better understanding of the hierarchy of the kingdom. You are keenly aware that you have been shaken but not uprooted. You are still standing. You have gained first hand experience. You have the ability to effectively encourage and strengthen others through the Tsunamis of their life.

And the Lord said, Simon, Simon, behold, Satan hath desired to have you that he may sift you as wheat: But I have prayed for thee, that thy faith fail not: And when thou are converted, strengthen thy brethren.
Luke 22:31-32 KJV

Chapter 24

Don't Forget the Important Stuff

We live in a world of advanced technology. We can connect with people face to face instantaneously from the comfort of our couch without ever picking up a phone. The Internet, video and other technology enables us to perform almost any kind of transaction from any where in the world. No matter where you go, you see people, young and old mesmerized by their technology. Smart phones, tablets, and other wireless devices are an integral part of our culture. Blue tooth seems to have become an extension of our ear.

Smart technology is interwoven in the mainstream of our culture. Both the young and old are proud users of smart technology. Grandparents are emailing and texting. Video technology enables us to see real time images of the person that we are speaking with on the phone. Photo albums have become extinct as we view pictures on our high definition televisions. Toddlers are indoctrinated in smart technology before they are even potty trained.

While dining in a restaurant, I saw a little girl who looked no older than three years of age. I watched her play with what I thought was an electronic game device. Upon closer examination, I noticed it was an I-Phone. I thought surely her mom let her play with the I-Phone to keep her occupied while she placed the food order. I was surprised when I saw her mother remove her own phone from her purse to make a call. I peered closer thinking perhaps the phone the child had was not working. To my disbelief, the phone worked and it belonged to the toddler. I watched her mom put the phone in the child's backpack when their meal arrived.

Most people will have one of two reactions to this story; 1) you are in shock and saddened, as I was, or 2) you think it is perfectly normal that a toddler needs that type of technology. Before going further, let me state that I am grateful for the technology that is available to us today. However, I am equally disturbed by the grip it has on our lives. It is a double-edged sword. For as much as technology is a blessing, it can also be a curse. We allow technology to rob us of real human interaction.

I wonder how our lives would change if we laid down our gadgets for one day. Imagine what it would feel like to spend dedicated quality time with family and friends. Consider how important your spouse and kids would feel if you turned off your devices and actually talked with them during dinner. You have the opportunity to create wonderful memories by playing with your kids instead of relying upon a game to entertain and babysit them. Imagine how much more fulfilling our lives would be if we decided to have rule over technology instead of it ruling over us.

We are overlooking the really important stuff. Electronic devices have robbed us of hours and maybe even years from our lives. Perhaps this is what was meant when it was said that there would be a day when machines would rule the world.

Take time to unplug. Step out of the virtual world into reality. A computer generated rose appears perfect in it's beauty; but nothing can compare to the velvety softness and sweet fragrance of a freshly cut rose. Don't forget the important stuff. Stop and smell the roses.

The thief cometh not, but for to steal and to kill and to destroy: I am come that they might have life, and that they might have it more abundantly.
John 10:10 KJV

Chapter

25

When God Is Silent, or so You Think He Is

At some time or another we all have experienced the silent treatment. Remember those times when you or your spouse put forth that very special effort to ignore one another to get your point across. It's our way of making them hear us. Funny, isn't it? We become silent so that we can be heard.

There are pivotal points in our lives where we experience what feels like the silent treatment from God. There are times when you pray, searching for direction that will give you peace, comfort and assurance. God does not speak to you. It feels like God's silent treatment lasts for an eternity. We struggle to grasp the mystery of what is happening in our life. We focus our attention, desperately wanting to hear God's voice. We look for him in the quiet hours, through the voice of the preacher, our prayers and the written word. We are looking for that one word that will make sense of the things that are troubling our hearts. Still there is no response; or so it seems. We are forced to wait quietly for an answer. We trust that God is with us and will give the clarity that we are desperately in need of.

Let's reflect upon what happens during the silent treatment:

1) God gets our attention. Our life is out of balance. We are acutely aware when we cannot readily hear him. When we cannot discern the voice of God, we long for his reassurance.
2) We whole-heartedly seek God's direction and guidance for our life.
3) We are cognizant of the void that is felt when we cannot hear God. We are equally cognizant of the fact that we really don't know what to do without his direction.
4) We learn patience as we continue to wait for the one word from the Lord that will deliver us from the trial we are experiencing.
5) We are sober. We have a heightened awareness of how we interact with people throughout the course of our daily activities. We are both reserved and on guard.
6) We remember the Lord, reflecting upon our history with him. We remember the miracles God has

performed in our lives. We find encouragement and strength as we wait for him to answer.

7) Our faith matures. We transition from feeling to knowing that God is with us. We know that God is perfecting everything that concerns us, even when we don't understand.

It is a natural tendency to think we should have a seat at the table with God when it concerns our lives. In reality, that is as foolish as consulting a two year old on financial planning.

We all want to go from faith to faith and glory to glory, as long as we can map out the path. If it were up to us, we would never get there. Jesus clearly understood hierarchy and order when he told his Father, "O my Father, if it be possible, let this cup pass from me; nevertheless not as I will, but as thou wilt" (Matthew 26:39 KJV).

I don't know about you, but I can't imagine volunteering to go through pain, suffering, loss of loved ones and trials. I would suggest alternative learning methods to the Lord. I would try to convince him to let me attend a class or complete an on-line study program. I would argue that I did not need the actual experience and that I could learn from case studies provided through the course curriculum. Can you fathom the

CEO of a company asking your permission to make a business decision? Yet we want the creator to consult the creation.

I am continuously reminded that God is sovereign. He planned my life before the foundation of the earth. I am in his hands. I experience faith-to-faith and glory-to-glory moments as I am propelled into a higher dimension in him. I will embrace the silent treatment declaring, even as Jesus did, "Nevertheless, not as I will, but as thou wilt."

> *For I know the thoughts that I think toward you, says the Lord, thoughts of peace and not of evil, to give you a future and a hope.*
> *Jeremiah 29:11 NKJV*

Chapter 26

Life Is Like a Seesaw

I remember as a child during recess racing with my friend to play on the seesaw. We would laugh and enjoy one another as we happily propelled each other up and down from the ground. No one ever told me that the seesaw would be like life, full of ups and downs.

As a child, I fantasized about adult life and played it out in my mind over and over, and yes, over again. I don't remember imagining anything less that a perfect fairy tale life. Though I have experienced some fairy tale moments; my life has been anything but a fairy tale. If anything, my life can be compared to a quote from the movie Forrest Gump when Tom Hanks said, "Life is like a box of chocolates, and you never know what you are going to get inside."

I have come to appreciate and even embrace both the ups and downs. Even though the downs can sometimes knock you off of your feet, they are often the launching pad that propels you up towards your destiny. Your downs are the foundation of your greatness.

Let us consider:

Oprah Winfrey faced many hardships during her childhood years. Oprah became an iconic voice to people around the world. She is one of the most influential and wealthiest women in the world.

John Walsh, authored three best-selling books, became one of the most renown human and victim's rights advocate when his six year-old son, Adam, was abducted and murdered. The National Center for Missing and Exploited Children was created to protect children and provided resources to parents, children and law enforcement worldwide.

Nancy Goodman Brinker lost her sister, Susan Komen to breast cancer at the age of thirty-six in 1982. She founded the Susan G. Komen for the Cure in 1982. This non-profit organization is a world-renowned organization in education, prevention and research for the cure of breast cancer.

People generally become famous when they have achieved an "up" milestone in life that garners attention from the media.

We see them in their glamour and notoriety. I have been fortunate to meet several well-known, accomplished people. In my conversations with them, I don't ask about things I can research on the Internet. I ask about their "down" experiences and the toughest lessons learned. This type of question causes a person to stop and reflect over their journey. Not surprisingly, each response that has been shared has been a pivotal "down" experience that has played an integral part in propelling the person to their current success and notoriety.

The majority of people that achieve some level of greatness will tell you that to truly appreciate what they have accomplished, you have to understand where they have come from. It is through my own ups and downs that I can share my journey in a small way to help you through the seesaw of life.

I know how to be abased, and I know how to abound: everywhere and in all things I have learned both to be full and hungry, both to abound and to suffer need. I can do all things through Christ, which strengthens me.
Philippians 4:12-13 NKJV

Chapter 27

Eyes Wide Open

Look around you. What do you see? Is what you see real or is your vision distorted? If you see a glass that is filled at fifty percent capacity, is it half full or half empty? Our worldview is shaped by our knowledge and experiences.

Just imagine with me, a mother of an only child who has been missing for several weeks opening her door to a police officer. She looks desperately into his eyes. As he speaks to her, she clutches her blouse, crying uncontrollably she falls to her knees. This captures the attention of her neighbor who was observing from across the street. The neighbor looks on, as the officer appears to try and console the woman. The woman clings to the officer still sobbing.

What does the neighbor see? What would you see? Do you see tragedy or an expression of joy? Was the officer the bearer of bad news or a messenger of joy?

We view God in a very similar way. We write the story of who God is from the snapshot of our limited knowledge and experience. Our foundation was formed by the teachings of the patriarchs and matriarchs that have gone before us. We are a new generation church and have exceeded those that have gone before us. We have had experiences with God that has lulled us into thinking that we can readily recognize him. We have become familiar. We grant God permission to be sovereign within the scope of our worldview.

We have everything worked out. Everything fits perfectly into our plan. We are right on schedule and without warning we experience a spiritual earthquake. It is the type of shaking that will force a separation of the wheat from the chaff in your own belief system. Some may refer to it as a Job experience.

This is the experience where you learn that you were disillusioned. It is the refining process. It is a painful process that separates impurities out of every aspect of your life. You learn that scales have been on your eyes distorting your vision. God performs laser surgery. He removes the haze from your eyes. Your eyesight is clean and crisp. Your vision is perfect. You can see the smallest of details. You are elated and grieved. You are humbled by the reality of the years you were misguided and are overwhelmed by the clarity of vision you have received from God. Your vision is no longer clouded by false teachings. It is based upon a fresh experience with God. It is intimate. It belongs to you and God. You can see clearly now.

I have heard of you by the hearing of the ear; but now my eye sees you.
Job 42:5 NKJV

Chapter 28

Artificial Glory

It has been said that fear is false evidence appearing real. This is my definition of artificial glory. It is false evidence that appears real. Artificial glory produces unsustainable fruit that appeals to your emotions. It is based upon what you see. It gives the appearance of the real thing, but upon closer examination, it is just a vapor. Like steam from a boiling pot of water; it quickly disappears when the heat is turned off.

Artificial glory is manifested in a variety of ways. We've seen it often in the church when we glorify man rather than God. We have seen several ministers of the gospel fall from a place of honor. Some have become victims of artificial glory. We inflate their egos with misplaced praise. We ignore their humanity when we idolize them making them deities through our admiration.

Artificial glory shows up in businesses. It is cloaked in politics and the good old boy network. Artificial glory manifests in small-minded people with big titles. A person under this cloud is easy to spot. Some of the characteristics include the misuse of authority, selfishness and poor leadership. Employees often become collateral damage under leadership that is a product of artificial glory.

The cloud of artificial glory plagues our celebrities and athletes. This toxic cloud of glory rapidly takes them to the highest of heights, only to be followed by the fall to the deepest of lows when the glory has evaporated.

The most dangerous type of artificial glory is self-deceit. It is manifested in pride and ignorance. It is self-serving inflicting hurt and discomfort to others. It is judgmental and its main purpose is self-elevation. Like carbon monoxide, it is odorless, tasteless and invisible to the naked eye, but make no mistake, it is lethal.

Artificial glory can be discerned. Sometimes it is easily recognized, other times it has to be unveiled. There are always signs that artificial glory is present. There are two identifying factors:

   1) It is temporal – it has no staying power, and

2) It is ultimately exposed as an imposter – it is never what you believed it was. It's like a cubic zirconia being presented as a diamond. When it is examined under a jeweler's eye, you discover that it is worthless.

Artificial glory is impotent. It is counterfeit. We must give care that we are not lulled into embracing artificial glory. True glory is of God. His glory brings eternal change. By his glory, the Israelites were led from Egypt. By his glory, they were sustained for forty years in the desert. By his glory nations were built and destroyed.

God's presence comes with his glory. In his presence darkness is destroyed. In his presence you experience the fullness of his glory. His glory permanently transforms your spirit and life. When you experience the real glory of God it is easier to recognize artificial glory. Trust me, there is nothing like the real glory of God.

Who is the King of Glory? The Lord strong and mighty. The Lord mighty in battle. Lift up your heads, O ye gates; even lift them up, ye everlasting doors, and the King of Glory shall come in. Who is the King of Glory? The Lord of Hosts, He is the King of Glory. Selah.

Psalm 24:8-10 KJV

Chapter 29

Positioning Does Not Equal Sovereignty

We learn early how to position ourselves in almost all aspects of our life. People strive for positions in school, church, organizations and the like. There are literally thousands of books that offer strategies about positioning yourself in your career, finances, business deals and much more. One of the most familiar strategies is called networking. Networking allows people to connect with other people specifically to meet, exchange information and establish connections, usually for self-serving purposes. There are actual meetings and events that are designed to promote networking. Some people carefully select organizations to volunteer their service with the intent of networking to position himself or herself in the community, a particular trade or industry.

This is not a surprise nor is it a new trend. People have been trying to position themselves since the days of Christ. Do you remember the woman who asked Jesus to seat her son at his right hand? The right hand represented strength and power.

It happens in ministry. People jockey for high exposure positions in the church. Sadly, there are people that join a church with the intent of positioning themselves with a particular part of the ministry for personal gain rather than service. I attended a church service where a misinformed pastor told the congregation that God would only bless them through him and that the people would never be blessed beyond him. In this case, the pastor positioned himself equal with God. I'm not sure which saddened me the most, the disillusioned pastor's comments or the resounding "amen'" that came from the congregation.

When people can't obtain a desired position, they will create one. The best example of someone trying to create his own position is Lucifer. The scriptures read that Lucifer said in his heart, "I will ascend into heaven, I will exalt my throne above the stars of God: I will sit also upon the mount of the congregation in the sides of the north; I will ascend above the heights of the clouds; I will be like the most High" (Isaiah 14:13 KJV). Talk about positioning gone wrong! We all know how that worked out for Satan. He not only lost his position as chief worshipper among the angels, he was cast into the pit of hell along with one third of the angels he had deceived. This really gives us something to think about. Are you attaching yourself to someone that you believe is positioned to elevate you? You may want to re-evaluate.

The most important thing to know about positioning is that it means you are out of position; you haven't attained the spot. People often try to secure something that they have no control over. It is usually not meant for them because they don't have the capacity to handle it. We must know who we are and even more importantly, we must know who we are not. As we strive to attain positions, it is noteworthy to remember that people and positions change.

For example, in large corporations, the first thing a new CEO does is to move out the old regime. He brings in a team of people that he trusts and has a prior relationship. I have watched executives with more than twenty years of experience be removed from positions while new people are placed in their position before the ink is dry on the severance agreement. There is a lesson to be learned. Man-made or man-appointed positions are temporal and can be eliminated with the stroke of a pen.

Let's consider positioning with God. We migrate through several positions with God. First, we are born into a position of sin. We are sinners. We execute the responsibilities of this position without any formal training.

The next position is conversion. Conversion occurs when a person accepts Jesus Christ as Lord and Savior. Once converted, one generally assumes the position of practicing religion based upon the belief in Jesus Christ. In this position, behavioral changes occur as the person learns the ways of a Christian. There are some that stay in this position. Typical characteristics of this religious position include church attendance, praying, volunteerism, increase in giving and adherence to the laws of the land. Religion is sometimes confused with denominations. Denominations typically define how you practice your religious belief. You may have been asked, "What religion are you?" It would be more accurately asked, "What is your religious positioning?"

For those that move beyond the position of religion, the next level of positioning is being born again. In this position one experiences the baptism of the Holy Spirit. This is a transitional position where one goes from religion to relationship. You move through many levels in this position. These levels can be viewed as faith-to-faith and glory-to-glory. Each level brings a deeper understanding and relationship with the Lord. The first stage, as Paul referred to it, is the milk stage. It is the position of being a babe in Christ. This is such an exciting stage. God reveals himself. The word is made alive. Everything is new. You see things you have never seen. You observe the smallest of miracles. You are in awe of God. In this position the mystery of the Word is revealed. You see and understand with clarity. You are able to grasp the wonder of God and His Word. This is such a wonderful position in Christ.

The next stage can be referred to as meat. In this position you are weaned from milk and are given meat. Your spiritual awareness and understanding is enlightened. You are growing in Christ. You develop a level of maturity in the things of God. Occasionally, you may revert back to the milk stage but only for a short season before returning back to the meat stage. In this position you grow and mature. You learn to be accountable for your actions and things concerning God. A person may discover his or her purpose in this position. We stay in this position for a long time, for there is much to be learned and mastered. We pass some exams but fail a lot more. It is all part of the learning process. After God has refined us we are ready to advance to a more senior position.

This senior level position can be referred to as seasoned. In this position you have navigated through many different seasons in your life. You have experienced suffering, loss, disappointment and pain. These experiences have birthed wisdom and knowledge in your life. You have an in-depth understanding of God's word. You understand that God is sovereign. You are not moved by your emotions and have gained a keen ability to put life in perspective. You focus on what matters, understanding that God is in control. It is in this senior level position that you are able to extend the wisdom of lessons learned to help others migrate through the many positions in God. You become the Teacher's Aide. You are able to offer guidance and instruction to others through your experiences on this journey with Christ.

Along the way, you will experience many levels and many positions in Christ. You can be certain that each position has a purpose and that there are lessons you will learn along the way. You won't have to jockey for a position or even a promotion. The position he created for you is yours and yours alone. It always has been, even before you were born. Don't try to jump into the position before you are ready, allow God groom you and place you in position at the appointed time.

Thus Jesse made seven of his sons pass before Samuel. And Samuel said to Jesse, "The Lord hath not chosen these." And Samuel said to Jesse, "Are all the young men here?" Then he said, "There remains yet the youngest, and, there he is keeping the sheep." And Samuel said to Jesse, "Send and bring him: for we will not sit down till he come here." So he sent and brought him in. Now he was ruddy, with bright eyes, and good looking. And the Lord said, "Arise, anoint him: for this is the one."

1Samuel 16: 10 – 12 NKJV

Chapter 30

Called by His Name

We respond differently when different people call us by name. Our responses differ based upon who is calling us and how we are called. I remember when I was a little girl my mother called me by my middle name. Sometimes I would be so busy at play my mother would have to call me two or three times before I would respond. It was a different story when she called me by my first and middle name. It was a different tone and I knew she meant business. I immediately wondered what I had done wrong. Thoughts would race through my mind as to what infraction I had committed as I hurried to respond to her call. Sometimes that call was for correction. Other times my mother had a gift or goodies for me. It did not matter which, when I heard my first and middle name, I responded immediately.

As I reflect over my life in the Lord, I smile because I have done him the exact same way. There have been times that the Lord has had to call me over and over before I would answer him. I was testing him to see just how much I could continue doing what I wanted to do without completely crossing the line. After several calls, I would reluctantly turn from playing and respond to his call. Then there are those times, I have heard the Lord's call and I knew he was only going to call my name once. Those are the times I have made haste in responding to the Lord. And like with my mother, sometimes those calls were for correction and other times they were for blessings.

The most interesting and wonderful thing is that regardless of correction or blessing, each call was for my benefit. Each call brought forth a learning experience that I would use later in life. The calls that led to correction did not feel good, nor did I like them. After all, I don't think I know anyone, adult or child, that likes correction. We may appreciate it, but we don't like it.

Sometimes when the Lord calls it is for instruction. When you move in obedience to the instruction of the Lord extraordinary things happen. Most times what the Lord has required of you seems crazy. Do you remember when the Lord spoke to Abraham about he and Sarah having a child? They were both well over ninety years of age. The Bible recorded that Sarah laughed within herself. The Bible is filled with rich history of the Lord giving his people what seemed to be absurd directives.

I had been promoted into a newly created position in my company. Although, I knew my boss, I did not have a personal relationship with him. Within days of accepting the position, I had to travel with my boss to Minneapolis where we would meet with a vendor to discuss a new endeavor. The trip was awkward and we both struggled to make small talk as we learned more about each other.

We arrived at the hotel, checked in and returned to the lobby where we would be joined by the vendor for dinner. They arrived promptly. We exchanged pleasantries and departed for dinner. The account executive, his regional vice president, my boss and I were seated outside on the patio of this very upscale restaurant with dishes on the menu that I had never heard of before. I listened to the conversation as they talked about affluent people that they all knew. I sat quietly smiling occasionally as I listened. Somehow the conversation shifted to church and my pastor's name came up. All eyes at that table shifted to me as they inquired about our charismatic ministry. And then it happened. I looked around the table and saw that they were all mesmerized as I spoke about the Holy Spirit and the gift of speaking in tongues. I explained to them that the gift of tongues is yet another language and answered their questions throughout the evening. They had spent the evening talking about all of the affluent powerful people they each knew. It was my turn. Of all of the people they had mentioned that evening, they had only heard of Jesus. They did not really know him. As I shared things that the Lord placed in my heart, I was reminded of children when they meet an iconic athlete or celebrity. They soaked in every word over the next hour or so.

When I returned to my room later that night, it dawned on me that I had spent the evening with my new boss and two new business acquaintances talking about the Holy Spirit and speaking in tongues. I would have to attend a meeting with them the very next morning. Surely, they must have thought that I was crazy. For a brief moment I considered that I had made a fool of myself. At this point, all I could do was tell the Lord that I had done what he instructed and go to sleep. It was too late and nothing could be retracted. There was no room for a do-over.

Little did I know that the conversation held over dinner would lay the foundation for the relationship with my boss over the course of the next year. My boss was a very logical, confident and smart man. He was on the fast track to an executive vice president position. He was powerful and someone that if you crossed it would mean career suicide. That, very awkward, dinner conversation on that warm night in August had set the tone of our relationship. Somewhere along the way our roles were reversed. I became his spiritual mentor. We had many conversations. He would tell me that every time we spoke he would have to go away and think about our discussions. He called me his counselor. During the course of the year, he softened and began to understand that there were more important things than climbing a career ladder. He saw the value of investing himself into something that was bigger than him. He retired. In one of our final conversations he told me that he was going to find out what he was supposed to be doing so that he could make a difference in the lives of others. To think, it all started with a conversation about the Holy Spirit and speaking in tongues during a business dinner.

When you are called by his name it is always prudent to answer, "Yes Lord," no matter how foolish it may seem. You never know whose life may be dependent upon your responsiveness.

And we know that all things work together for good to them that love God, to them who are the called according to his purpose.

Romans 8:28 KJV

Chapter 31

The Lord Is

The title of this chapter says it all; "The Lord Is." I remember one night many years ago I was studying my Bible and came upon the very noteworthy twenty-third Psalm. As I read those first three little words, tears streamed my face. I considered the majesty of the Lord. I thought about who he had been in my life. He was my transformer; he was whatever I needed at that moment. I marveled at how a seemingly invisible God was so very visible in every aspect of my life.

If you can imagine with me what Lois Lane must have felt like knowing that Superman would show up and rescue her from whatever crisis she found herself in, always in the nick of time. Think about how secure and protected she felt as he swooped her away to safety in his powerful arms.

For some, this might bring back fond childhood memories. It makes me smile as I consider those three little words, "The Lord Is." You see the Lord is truly everything to me. I can truly relate to the Apostle Paul when he wrote, "For in him we live, and move and have our being...." (Acts 17:28 KJV). I could never imagine my life without the Lord at the helm. I could tell you that the Lord is my healer, provider, comforter, protector, friend and so on. He is indeed all of those things, but he is so much more. Like many years ago, today when I consider those three little words, I still find myself in awe. Throughout the years, I have come to learn that the most I can imagine that the Lord is will be the least that he will ever be. My description of who the Lord is will always fall short. However, I am content in knowing that wherever I am, no matter the situation or the need, "The Lord Is." Who is he to you?

The Lord is my shepherd; I shall not want. He makes me to lie down in green pastures. He leads me beside still waters. He restores my soul. He leads me in the paths of righteousness for his name's sake. Even though I walk through the valley of the shadow of death, I will fear no evil for you are with me; your rod and your staff they comfort me. You prepare a table before me in the presence of my enemies, you anoint my head with oil; my cup overflows. Surely goodness and mercy shall follow me all the days of my life and I shall dwell in the house of the Lord forever.

Psalm 23:1-6 ESV

Conclusion

As we end our time together, let us acknowledge the sovereignty of God by declaring that "The Lord Is." As you close this book and continue your journey, always know that the Lord will guide you through every challenge you must face.

I have chosen to be transparent and shared some of my most intimate experiences with you hoping that you will be encouraged, inspired and healed. I pray that you received answers and reassurance.

My parting advice to you is to spend time in the presence of the Lord. Take time to enjoy life, your family and friends. Focus on things that really matter. Equally important, forgive yourself. We all need a "do-over" from time to time.

Know that you are not alone. Learn the lessons on your journey. There is someone waiting for you to strengthen them. You have a story within you that is waiting to be told.

Notes

Holy Bible English Standard Version ©2001 Crossway Bibles, a division of Good News Publishers

Holy Bible King James Version ©1999 Thomas Nelson, Inc.

New King James Version ©1981 Thomas Nelson, Inc.

New Living Translation, ©1996, 2004 Tyndale Charitable Trust, Tyndale House Publishers

www.amw.com/about_amw/John_Walsh.cfm

www.Komen.org